CREATIVE SKETCHBOOK *Magic*

CREATIVE SKETCHBOOK *Magic*

30 EASY & JOYFUL LESSONS TO UNLOCK THE ARTIST WITHIN

VIDDHI SASCHIT

BETTER DAY BOOKS®
HAPPY • CREATIVE • CURATED

Publisher: Peg Couch
Cover Designer: Michael Douglas
Book Designer: Llara Pazdan
Editor: Colleen Dorsey

ISBN: 978-0-7643-6947-6
Printed in India
10 9 8 7 6 5 4 3 2 1

Published by Better Day Books, an imprint of Schiffer Publishing, Ltd.

MIX
Paper | Supporting responsible forestry
FSC™ C016779

BETTER DAY BOOKS®

SCHIFFER PUBLISHING

Better Day Books
Email: hello@betterdaybooks.com
Web: www.betterdaybooks.com
Visit us on Instagram!
@better_day_books

Schiffer Publishing
4880 Lower Valley Road
Atglen, PA 19310
Phone: 610-593-1777
Fax: 610-593-2002
Email: info@schifferbooks.com
Web: www.schifferbooks.com

For our complete selection of fine books on this and related subjects, please visit our website at www.betterdaybooks.com. You may also write for a free catalog.

Better Day Books titles are available at special discounts for bulk purchases for sales promotions or premiums. Special editions, including personalized covers, corporate imprints, and excerpts, can be created in large quantities for special needs. For more information, contact the publisher.

DEDICATION

For my sweet daughter, who shared each moment of writing this book with me, growing inside my womb. This book holds a piece of her, my constant inspiration and joy.

Contents

PART 1: Getting Started

PART 2: Projects

PART 3: Taking Your Sketchbooking Further

Welcome!

If you want to develop your creativity and enhance your creative energy in a fun and easy way, starting with a sketchbook is for you! This book aims to help you connect with the purest form of your own creative energy, which is playful and joyful, even if it's your first time painting.

Through this book and the 30 tutorials it includes, you will gain insights and perspectives on creative energy, learning how to let it flow and how to become a channel for it. You'll also discover how to cultivate a daily painting practice that will ground you and encourage your creativity to flourish without pressure.

I can confidently tell you all this because sketchbook practice is something that I personally have turned to at different stages in my own creative journey—and my recent return to it is what sparked this book!

At the beginning of 2024, I made a decision to reintroduce a regular sketchbook practice into my life. In recent years, I had been focused on sharing my art in different ways—as original pieces, in surface pattern design collections, and through courses and online classes. While I was and am grateful to have had the chance to inspire others in these ways, I felt a deep need to nourish my own creativity. I wanted to create art for the pure joy of it, without any goals or pressures, just like in the early days of my artistic journey.

So, I started making daily painting a priority. I began each morning by filling blank pages in my sketchbooks with no agenda other than to explore and enjoy the process. Though I didn't plan on recording my sketchbook sessions, I occasionally shared small snippets of my work. To my surprise, this led to new opportunities! The joy I poured into my art connected with others, bringing in wonderful clients and eventually leading to an opportunity to host a sketchbook challenge.

Later, during a casual chat with the team at Better Day Books, who published my first book, *Gorgeous Gouache*, we exchanged ideas about the possibility of writing a second book to inspire people to build a regular creative practice. It felt like it was the perfect time for me to focus on writing, especially since I was pregnant and currently using sketchbook painting as a relaxing daily therapy. This way, I could work on my second book while still enjoying my personal creative time.

And that's how the book that you're holding in your hands came to existence. Who knew that by simply following my heart at the start of the year, everything would unfold like this by the end?

I hope this story inspires you to embrace creativity and commit to doing it for the pure joy of it, letting everything else unfold naturally while you're having fun. Wouldn't that be amazing? I wholeheartedly wish that the best unfolds for you as you tap into the creative joy of making sketchbook magic.

Viddhi Saachit

Meet Viddhi

We sat down with Viddhi to learn a little more about her and her artistic journey. Join us!

Hello! Tell us a little about yourself.

Hello, I'm Viddhi Saschit, a passionate, multi-faceted artist, surface-pattern designer, and mother to my daughter. My creative journey encompasses teaching art, designing patterns, creating fine-art paintings, and constantly exploring new ways to express myself. At the heart of my work is the intention to radiate joy and positivity through vibrant colors. I'm based in Chennai, India, and I hold deep beliefs and perspectives on the power of creativity.

What is it like where you live?

As a new mother, I absolutely love spending time in my studio. It's my peaceful retreat where I can immerse myself in creativity while my daughter enjoys her independent playtime. I live in a coastal area of my country—in fact, I live in a city with a beach, which is perfect, because I love beaches. Visiting the beach is my favorite thing to do nearby, but when I'm at home, I spend most of my time in my cozy home-studio office. Filled with beautiful colors and my paintings, it's a space that nurtures my creativity and brings me joy. It's the perfect balance—I'm able to watch my daughter grow and explore while having space to focus on my craft.

Besides art, what are your passions?

I'm passionate about inspiring and uplifting fellow creatives in a holistic way by sharing my story, thoughts, and experiences. I truly believe that a holistic approach is key to the growth of any artist, extending beyond just technical skills. It's about nurturing the right mindset and approaching creative energy with care and intention. Outside of my creative work, I love traveling with my little family, discovering new places, and testing out vegan recipes.

What do you love most about practicing in a sketchbook?

The most magical thing about my sketchbook is that it's a space where I can create without boundaries or judgment, simply enjoying the act of making art. It's a place for growth, joy, and play, which is why I cherish my sketchbook practice so much. Letting my ideas flow freely, without judgment, turns it into a powerful space for self-expression and personal growth. My sketchbook is not just a book—it's an extension of myself.

What do you hope people take away from this book?

I hope this book inspires people to create more art and unlock their endless creativity in a fun and effortless way! Whether you are a beginner or an experienced artist, this book will help you tap into your creative energy through playful exercises and inspiring prompts. It's about making art a daily practice, finding joy and peace in the process, and reconnecting with your inner child.

What is your advice to a beginner?

My advice to a beginner is this: you don't need to be a professional or know everything to make art. Just start where you are and allow yourself to explore. Art isn't about making something perfect or polished—it can be anything you want it to be. Many people believe they need to be skilled at painting or using brushes and colors to create art, but that's not true. Talent isn't a requirement. Everything can be learned over time, but you have to start somewhere—even if it's just with colorful lines and shapes. All you really need is the desire to create and to approach it with playfulness and joy, and the rest will follow naturally.

Viddhi Saschit is a deeply passionate artist and surface-pattern designer known for her joyful designs and positive energy. As a mother, she strives to balance her family life with her career, infusing her work with love and creativity. Her bright, colorful designs are licensed by brands around the world. Viddhi is the founder of Colour & Joy, a surface-pattern design company, and she has inspired more than 25,000 students through her creative workshops and Skillshare art classes. Viddhi is also the author of *Gorgeous Gouache*, holds a degree in architecture, and currently resides in Chennai, India. Learn more about her work at www.colourandjoy.in or connect with her on Instagram @viddhi.saschit or via email: hello@viddhisaschit.com.

I hope you get a lot of enjoyment from this book. If you do, you should check out my gouache instruction book, *Gorgeous Gouache*!

Creativity and Sketchbooks

Why choose a sketchbook to begin (or continue) your creative journey?

For me, sketchbooks have always been the safest space to freely express my creativity without judgment or the need for external validation. They offer a personal, no-pressure environment where you can experiment with colors, shapes, and techniques without worrying about the final outcome. Unlike loose sheets of paper, a sketchbook's pages feel like a continuous space where every mark is part of the creative process, and in one, there's no need to create something polished or "finished."

A sketchbook is a sanctuary for exploration, where mistakes are simply opportunities to learn and grow. The joy of sketching is in the act itself, not in the result. It's a place for pure play and self-expression, where you can let your ideas flow freely, without expectations. This space can also become a record of your journey, showing how your style or thoughts evolve over time. For me, the sketchbook is more than just a tool—it's an extension of myself, a powerful space for growth, joy, and creative exploration.

I remember when I first began my creative journey and started painting, I picked up a

Painting in a sketchbook provides natural inspiration to create more art; you don't need anyone to encourage or inspire you.

sketchbook and took my time filling its pages with colors and ideas. There was no pressure to make anything frame-worthy or suitable for gifting. It was just for me, a way to express myself freely and messily. From there, my creativity blossomed, eventually turning into a dream career.

Now, since 2017, I've maintained a sketchbook practice off and on as a way to return to my safe place. Every time I flip through my older sketchbooks, it brings me immense joy to see all the amazing art I've created. It's priceless to me, and it's one of the few things I get to keep forever without having to sell (as an artist). No matter where you are on your artistic journey, or where you go from here, the same will hold true for you.

Beyond the freedom that sketchbooks offer, the inspiration that radiates from each painted page will motivate you to create more art. Imagine flipping through the various filled pages of your sketchbook before you start on a new page; the previously painted pages will subconsciously inspire you to create. If you committed to sitting down and filling one page per day for 20 days, imagine how inspired and happy you would feel on day 21 when you see all the previous pages filled with creativity and gorgeous colors.

Through this book and its wonderful painting prompts, I hope you'll experience the magic of creativity, fall in love with making art, and stay inspired to keep creating. It's truly a magical practice to sit down with paints and brushes, exploring and expressing your inner child. I'm delighted to guide you on this magical journey through the pages of this book.

1

GETTING STARTED

Before you dive straight into the 30 projects, take some time to peruse the supply recommendations, basic techniques, and color guidance provided in the following pages. Your sketchbook is your own and has no rules, but, especially if you're a beginner, you may enjoy the confidence that reviewing the basics can bring you.

Basic Supplies

When it comes to sketchbooks, there are no rules or limits on supplies. You can use anything to explore creativity—oil pastel crayons, watercolor, acrylics, gouache, paint markers, inks, colored pencils, glitter pens, pigment liners, and more. It's all about letting your creativity run wild and free. While this book focuses on painting using gouache, watercolor, and acrylic paint markers, feel free to use any materials that inspire you. Just make sure that your sketchbook's paper is thick enough to handle whatever you throw at it—more detail on that below!

Sketchbook

Choose a watercolor or mixed-media sketchbook with a medium "tooth" or texture that has at least 30 pages. Pick a size that's comfortable for you—but I would not recommend going larger than letter size. My ideal size recommendation is 6" x 8" (A5) or a similarly sized square sketchbook. Both hardcover and softcover sketchbooks work fine; just make sure it's easy for you to lay the pages flat while you're painting.

Paintbrushes

Get a set of paintbrushes that are suitable for mixed media and that include an assortment of flat, round, and thin detail brushes. Soft, synthetic brushes work well for mixed media. Here are some size recommendations for your first few brushes; you can always add on from here!

- **Flat brush for background painting: ½" or 1"**
- **Round brush for multiple uses: size 6 or 8**
- **Round or liner brush for tiny details: size 0**

Paints

For painting in a sketchbook, there's no need to invest in professional-quality paints. If you already have them, great, but any quality supplies will work. The goal is to have fun and play with colors, and it's unlikely that you'll want to tear pages from your sketchbook to sell. (Always use professional-grade paints for artworks you do plan to sell!) When buying paints, look for brands that offer a good variety of colors, including bright hues as well as pastels.

Watercolors: Choose a set of 24 colors or more, either in tubes or cakes. They don't need to be expensive—budget-friendly options work just fine.

Gouache: A basic set of 12 or 24 colors is sufficient, and you can stick to budget-friendly options here as well.

Acrylic paint markers: You can invest in a small set of basic colors in a high-quality brand or purchase a set of 24–48 markers from a budget-friendly brand.

Miscellaneous Supplies

You'll need a container or glass to hold water, paper towels, colored pencils for sketching, gel pens, and pigment liners.

Painting Environment

Where you paint is not a supply you can purchase, but it's an important element to your process! When gathering supplies and setting up your painting space, keep it casual and inspiring. Create an environment that sparks joy and excitement. Use sticky notes or paint tiny posters with quotes that motivate you to create more art. If it's a possibility for you, painting outdoors can further enhance the joy of your creative practice, with fresh air and natural surroundings inspiring new perspectives.

Always approach your creative practice with the intention to experience joy and have fun. Let go of perfection and remember that sketchbooks are your safe space for learning, exploring, and making nonjudgmental art.

Watercolor Techniques

Watercolor is a fun and portable medium; it's one of my favorite choices because it's easy to use without creating a mess. Watercolor's special traits include:

- It's easily activated with water
- It can create both transparent and opaque effects
- Once dried on paper, it can't be reactivated with water

As a beginner, figuring out the right amount of water to use while painting can be a challenge. Don't give up—practice will help you get the hang of it. The water-to-paint ratio depends on various factors, including room temperature, which can also affect drying time, as well as the paper's quality, texture, and absorbency. After a few practice sessions, you'll become more comfortable.

Let's explore some basic watercolor techniques to help you get familiar with this medium.

Wet on Dry

For this technique, simply apply wet paint to dry paper. This technique gives you more control over the paint's flow.

Wet on Wet

This popular technique creates beautiful effects. Wet the paper with water or paint, then use a brush loaded with paint to drop color onto the wet surface. The paint spreads easily, creating soft blends. It's very easy to combine colors this way.

Dry Brushing

To achieve a textured effect, use a damp brush with minimal paint. Remove excess water with a paper towel, dip the brush into the paint, and gently drag it across the paper. This technique is great for adding final details and gives you fine control over where the paint goes.

Gradients

This technique is used to create a seamless blend of two colors. Pick any two colors and paint two swatches, with one color on top and one on the bottom with a gap between them. Next, rinse the color from the paintbrush and load the brush with water. Then move the brush from the top color down midway into the gap, repeat for bottom color, and then blend both colors in the center.

Values

To create lighter and darker variations of the same color, you can simply adjust the water-to-paint ratio. Start with a darker value and gradually add more water to make lighter shades. Take it all the way to pastel by using a lot of water and little paint.

An alternative way to make lighter values with watercolor is to mix in white paint, but keep in mind that adding white will reduce the paint's transparency, making the watercolor more opaque, similar to gouache.

Painting Tip

If your paint flows more than expected, it's likely due to excess water in your brush or paint. To manage this, tap your brush on the side of your water container or blot it on a paper towel before picking up paint. If your brush glides too smoothly and the paint spreads too easily, reduce the amount of water. Practicing this awareness will help you gain better control over your brushwork and achieve the desired effects in your painting.

Gouache Techniques

Gouache is a water-based medium that combines the qualities of watercolor and acrylic paints. It allows for adding multiple layers and fine details to a painting and dries thicker and more opaque than watercolors. Gouache's special traits include:

- **It's easily activated with water when moist**
- **It requires effort to reactivate once dried on the palette**
- **It dries with a velvety, matte finish**
- **It can create both transparent and opaque effects**

Store gouache paints in a moist environment. When squeezing paint from a tube, squeeze out only what you need. For paints in pans or tubs, seal them well to retain moisture; consider using a mold spray to prevent mold growth. Also note that once a finished piece of gouache work dries on paper, it still can be reactivated with water, so finished paintings should be stored carefully or sealed with spray varnish.

Let's explore some basic gouache techniques to help you get familiar with this medium.

Understanding Consistency

Too watery

Too thick

Right consistency

Wet on Dry

Wet on Wet

Color Lifting

Dry Brushing

Understanding Consistency

Understanding the consistency of gouache is key. If the paint is too thick, with very little water, it won't glide smoothly on the paper. Using too much water will dilute the paint, making it more transparent, like watercolor, and causing it to lose its unique characteristic opacity. Adding a lot of water can create a creamy texture, but the final result will have a mix of transparent and opaque areas. The ideal consistency has enough water to eliminate visible brushstrokes and to allow the paint to dry evenly with a solid, velvety finish.

As a beginner, finding the right water-to-paint ratio for gouache can be tricky. Don't get discouraged—practice will help you master it. The water ratio largely depends on the paint brand. Some gouache paints are very thick and need more water to activate, while others may be more fluid. A bit of experimentation will go a long way.

Wet on Dry

This technique involves applying wet paint to dry paper or an already dry layer of paint. It's commonly used for adding initial base layers as well as final details.

Wet on Wet

Ideal for covering large areas, this technique involves wetting a section of paper first, then applying wet paint to it. It's quite useful for creating background effects.

Color Lifting

This technique lifts paint from a previous layer to create a glowing effect. Apply a patch of color using the wet-on-dry technique, let it dry, and then use a damp brush to lift off some of the color, revealing some of the white paper (or previous color) underneath.

Dry Brushing

Dry brushing with gouache is similar to dry brushing with watercolor. Use a damp brush with thick paint and gently drag it across the paper. It's great for creating textured effects.

Painting Tip

To create pastel colors in gouache, simply add white to your chosen color!

Acrylic Paint Marker Techniques

Acrylic paint markers are fun and easy to use, with no mess involved. Simply use the paint pens to create art anywhere! They are thick acrylic paint markers filled with liquid acrylic paint, which is generally waterproof but not permanent. These markers are highly pigmented, making them suitable for both complete artworks and fine details. Acrylic paint markers' special traits include:

- **They have an opaque, flowing paint consistency**
- **They are best used on smooth paper surfaces to prevent damage to the marker tip**
- **They are ideal for layering and adding fine details**
- **They are ideal for lettering and writing quotes**

Acrylic paint markers come in one of two forms: brush markers or pump markers. Brush markers feature a pointed tip, allowing you to paint similarly to using a brush. Pump markers have a blunt tip and require initial pumping to get the paint flowing. Before using any acrylic paint marker, shake it thoroughly to ensure the paint flows evenly.

Let's explore some basic acrylic paint marker techniques to help you get familiar with this medium.

Basic Techniques

Non-Layering Technique

Layering Technique

Basic Techniques

Avoid zigzag strokes and refrain from painting too quickly. Also skip crisscross patterns—don't try to fill a space with crisscrossing lines. All these methods will more often than not end up oversaturating your paper without giving you good or even coverage. Instead, use long, even strokes that are placed closely together to create a smooth, uniform finish. Notice how closely spaced lines create a solid, even swatch of paint on the paper in the sample shown.

Non-Layering Technique

Try painting this simple potted plant without any layering.

1. **Draw the outline of the pot.**
2. **Fill it in with paint using longer strokes or lines.**
3. **Draw solid leaves and stems, then add simple dot flowers.**

Layering Technique

Now try painting a butterfly using layering. Whenever you layer acrylic paint markers, always wait to apply the next layer of paint once the previous layer has dried to avoid contaminating the marker tip with a different color.

1. **Paint a solid background using a lighter color. Remember to use long, even lines to cover the surface. Let dry.**
2. **Draw a simple butterfly body and wing outlines with dark colors, then fill in the wings. Let dry.**
3. **Use a fine-tipped black pen to add the antennae.**

A Creative Approach to Colors

Choosing colors is my favorite part of creating art. It's a therapeutic process to pick colors intuitively, adding extra joy to the creative experience. This is especially true when creating art in sketchbooks, where you're free to express your ideas and imagination without the pressure of perfecting a piece.

Traditionally, art classes and books teach color mixing using primary colors, which is a great way to learn about color theory. However, my approach is focused on experiencing joy through cultivating a creative practice rather than on mastering techniques. When you develop a daily practice, you will naturally gain a deeper understanding of colors.

This is how I became a master of colors—by exploring them daily in my sketchbook, rather than sticking to a traditional approach. This playful method allowed me to get creative without feeling overwhelmed by the dry theory of color mixing, helping me understand

Here are the colors I used most frequently in this book!

colors in my own way. Learning this way, through personal exploration, is what I recommend to you.

By easing the pressure of mixing the "right" colors, you can fully immerse yourself in the joy of creating. That's why, throughout this book, I've simplified color mixing and palettes for each project we'll paint together, so you can experience the true magic of creativity.

With all of this in mind, I will, in the next few pages, give you a very basic introduction to color theory and mixing so that you can choose how much you want to engage with it.

A Note About the Project Color Palettes

To help you fully enjoy the process of painting, I've simplified the color instructions for each of the 30 projects in this book. **My aim isn't for you to match the exact colors I used for each project**, but instead to help you experience the joy of creating art and develop a daily art practice that is easy, joyful, and free from overwhelm—a practice that will make you want to continue it every day. That's the true goal of this book.

Accordingly, in the projects, I'll use simple color terms like bright blue and orange. You can choose a color from your palette that's closest to these, or you can mix new colors on the basis of the color-mixing exercise (page 29). Occasionally, I'll provide specific color recipes for projects when I think it would be especially helpful. As always, feel free to swap in any color you prefer instead of sticking strictly to my suggestions!

Color Mixing

If you're completely new to making art and mixing colors, here are some tips to keep in mind.

- The specific ratio of two or three colors mixed together will determine the final result.
- Avoid mixing more than four colors, as the outcome often turns out dark and muddy.
- Start with small amounts of paint when mixing—it's easier to adjust the color by gradually adding more paint.
- Test your mixed colors on a scrap piece of paper before applying them to your artwork.
- If your water container is muddy and dark, it can dull your colors. Be sure to change your water frequently.

The Basics of Color Mixing

The primary colors are the three basic colors—red, yellow, and blue—that are used to mix a variety of colors. Blue and yellow make green, blue and red make purple, and red and yellow make orange.

On the facing page, you can see examples of how mixing primary colors in various ratios, along with white, can produce a very wide variety of different colors.

Primary Colors

Basic Color Mixing

Warm Colors

Cool Colors

Color Mixing and Exploring Exercise

It's important to complete this exercise before starting any of the projects in this book. So grab your paint medium—watercolor or gouache; it doesn't matter.

First, swatch all the existing colors in your palette on a sketchbook page. Then, pick pairs of colors, like red and yellow, blue and green, or red and blue. Mix them in different ratios on the paper and observe how they create a range of new colors. You'll be surprised by the variety you can achieve. You can also experiment by mixing three primary colors in different ratios to explore darker hues.

This exercise will help you understand how color mixing works. Focus on observing the process rather than writing down the colors you create—just enjoy it. You can always experiment again later to rediscover the shades you mixed. This approach helps you learn and master color mixing on your own, without relying on prewritten color recipes. Plus, it allows you to discover new colors naturally!

Experience the joy of mixing colors when you do this exercise.

Color Recipes

Apart from the color-mixing exercise on the previous page, I would love to share some of my favorite color mixes with you so that you can use them as you work on the projects in this book—or your own creations!

Vibrant Color Recipes

Pastel Color Recipes

Making Happy Color Palettes

Ever wondered why every work I create radiates sheer joy and happiness? Here is my secret.

I love expressing vibrant and soothing energy through my artwork, and you'll notice a blend of bright and pastel colors in every piece of work if you look closely. I tend to avoid using high-contrast colors like black—it's just a personal preference. Instead, when I need darker tones, I mix primary colors rather than using straight black. This approach creates a balanced, eye-pleasing effect in my work.

The example shown here will help you understand how to create happy color palettes like mine. The top palette shown is vibrant and pretty, but it includes a lot of contrasting colors. The bottom palette, however is still vibrant and pretty, but it's also soothing because it blends pastels and bright colors.

A nice palette

My kind of palette

Now, imagine a floral artwork painted with each of these two palettes. Which one do you think would look more pretty, happy, and calming? The second one, right? This is the art of balancing colors in a palette and making a happy color palette that radiates joy.

Color Palette Exercise

Choose a blank page in your sketchbook. Try to combine five to seven colors into a palette that you like. Then try again to create a fresh palette. Then try making a totally random palette. Use a scrap of paper to cover up other palettes and focus only on one single palette at a time to decide how much you like it. Experimenting with color palettes like this can be so much fun, and you can return to your color palette page any time to choose and use a premade palette for a piece of art!

find joy
in little
things

2 PROJECTS

Are you finally ready to start your daily creative practice? This section of the book contains 30 step-by-step projects to get you started with your first month of sketchbook work. The projects use watercolor, gouache, sometimes a blend of both, and sometimes incorporating acrylic paint markers. However, feel free to use any art mediums that inspire you. Focus on creating with joy!

Tropical Leaves

Let's paint some tropical leaves with a fun twist by adding some vibrant colors! Instead of just the usual green tones, we'll use breezy blues, bright pink, and lots of citrusy yellow and orange shades. While you're painting, focus on how these colors energize and rejuvenate you. And remember, feel free to choose your own color palette—the one below is just for reference.

Medium

Watercolor

Tools and Supplies

- Size 6 round paintbrush
- Thin liner paintbrush
- White acrylic paint marker
- Pencil

Color Palette

Permanent yellow

Opera pink

Peach*

Coral orange*

Pale blue

Pastel blue*

Ultramarine blue

Mixing Instructions

Peach: Dilute orange with water

Coral orange: A little red + pastel orange

Pastel blue: Dilute cerulean blue with water

1. Sketch. Using a pencil, lightly sketch a set of varied leaves. You can follow my drawing or make up your own set of leaves.

2. Paint. For the monstera leaf and two solid leaves, wet the paper, then drop in various colors using the wet-on-wet technique. Notice how each color blends into another. For the other elements, paint each leaf with a single color.

3. Add detail. Use ultramarine blue to paint the leaf veins and to add a bit of shadow around the edges of the monstera leaf.

4. Get creative! You can add color to the background, use a white acrylic paint marker for extra details, or doodle in the leaves with a fine-liner pen. Just have fun!

Free-Spirited Butterflies

Where there is one butterfly, there are many butterflies!
For this gorgeous project, you will get to practice by making a single butterfly first, then create a whole page of them with colorful details and interesting patterns. Let's get started on this pretty butterfly that's just as free-spirited as you!

Medium

Watercolor

Tools and Supplies

- Size 6 round paintbrush
- Thin liner paintbrush
- Pencil

Color Palette

Opera pink

Permanent yellow

Orange

Ultramarine blue

Teal blue

Peach*

Mixing Instructions

Peach: Dilute orange with water

1. Sketch. Using a pencil, lightly sketch the butterfly wings. You can follow my drawing or choose any butterfly shape you'd like.

2. Add initial color. Start by adding loose brushstrokes of different colors within the butterfly outline. Try to paint each of the wings of the butterfly with similar colors in similar spots so that the wings match.

3. Add detail. Add a second layer of brushstrokes using different colors to create patterns. Paint simple lines and dots on top of the solid colors and then paint the butterfly's body and antennae with ultramarine blue.

4. Paint more butterflies. Fill up the entire page with similar butterflies in different sizes. Dilute some paint to a watery consistency and tap the paintbrush from a few inches above the paper to create some splash effects.

Cozy Cats

Imagine cats in sweaters all cozied up during the snowy weather.
If you get some creative ideas for this prompt, feel free to explore them. You could paint a cozy cat snuggled up on a sofa, perched near a fireplace, or sitting by a window watching the snow! The wintry possibilities are endless.

Medium

Watercolor

Tools and Supplies

- Thin liner paintbrush
- Pencil

Color Palette

Mixing Instructions

Medium violet: Dilute violet with water

Pastel blue: Dilute cerulean blue with water

Peach: Dilute orange with water

1. Sketch. Using a pencil, lightly sketch three cats in different positions as shown. Give each one a scarf. Add some snowflakes around them.

2. Outline. Paint the outline of each cat in violet. Don't paint the snowflakes yet at all, though (unlike as shown in the image).

3. Add detail. Paint the scarves on the cats ultramarine blue. Then create a sweater pattern on each cat by painting some lines, dots, zigzags, etc. using different colors.

4. Add background. Add a soft wash of color beneath each cat to represent a floor or rug. When that is dry, go back in to add detail lines. Finally, paint snowflakes and add dots to represent snow.

Lettering Quote

Filling up pages in your sketchbook doesn't always need to involve a theme or particular object to paint. You can also fill up pages with an inspiring quote each day until you have a beautiful collection that you would love to be reminded of when you flip through your sketchbook. It can be a wonderful way to incorporate some art therapy into your morning routine.

Medium

Gouache

Tools and Supplies

- Size 6 round paintbrush
- Thin liner paintbrush
- Acrylic paint markers
- Pencil

Color Palette

Mixing Instructions

Peach: Orange + white

Pastel pink: Opera pink + white

Turquoise blue: Cerulean blue + permanent yellow + white

Pastel purple: Purple + white

1. Sketch. Using a pencil, lightly sketch your letters in a block style, making sure you make them big enough and wide enough to be able to fill them with color and pattern later.

2. Fill the letters. Using your round brush, paint every letter in a different color. You can also add multiple colors in the same letter for extra fun, such as the two-toned blue, purple, and orange letters I included here.

3. Add details. Using your thin liner brush, fill each letter by painting dark details on light letters and light details on dark letters, creating patterns like waves, lines, and dots. You can also use paint markers here instead of gouache if you prefer.

4. Add background. Now paint some fun shooting-star elements around the quote. Use your palette colors to paint various stars with streaming tails.

Boho Butterfly

We painted a butterfly earlier in this book, but since they're so fun to paint, here's another approach. It may seem very similar, but the process will feel different. This project will spark ideas for how to paint the same subject in several different ways. No sketching is required here, so we can jump right into painting. You can always sketch first if you'd like, but it's a great exercise to develop an organic shape of a butterfly with just paint.

Medium

Watercolor (or you can use gouache instead)

Tools and Supplies

- Size 6 (or your choice) round paintbrush
- Thin liner paintbrush

Color Palette

Permanent yellow
Pastel orange*
Coral orange*
Pastel purple*
Pastel blue*
Periwinkle*
Purple
Opera pink

Mixing Instructions

Pastel orange: Dilute orange with water
Coral orange: A little red + pastel orange
Pastel purple: Dilute purple with water
Pastel blue: Cerulean blue + white
Periwinkle: Purple + blue, then dilute with water

1. Start the shape. Paint the center of the butterfly, then add some brushstrokes in different colors in the shape of a butterfly's wings. Make the brushstrokes similar on each wing.

2. Add more color. Fill in more colors and paint brushstrokes on the edges of the wings to make them more defined.

3. Add details. Paint darker details on existing color areas, creating patterns like waves, lines, and dots. You can continue to adjust the shape of the wings too if you want.

4. Add a background. Add a background layer of peach behind the butterfly, leaving a thin halo of unpainted white outlining it.

Coral Reef

It's fascinating just how much color there is within aquatic life!
Let's paint a beautiful underwater coral landscape, exploring the different colors and textures that naturally occur. We'll use multiple values of various colors to represent texture and shadow, then we'll add some taller corals and filler elements in the background.

Medium

Watercolor

Tools and Supplies

- Size 6 round paintbrush
- Thin liner paintbrush
- Pencil

Color Palette

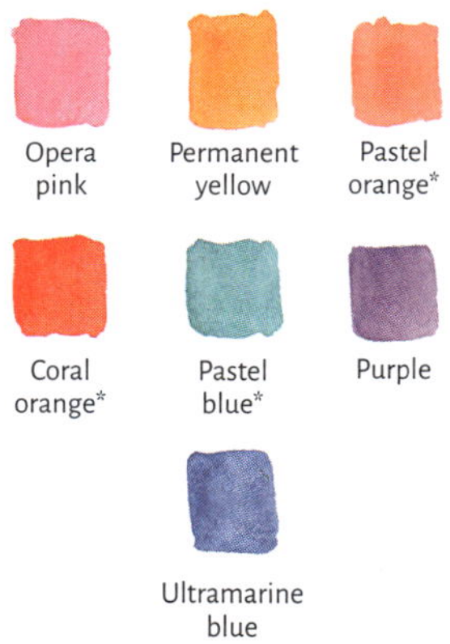

Mixing Instructions

Pastel orange: Dilute orange with water
Coral orange: A little red + pastel orange
Pastel blue: Dilute cerulean blue with water

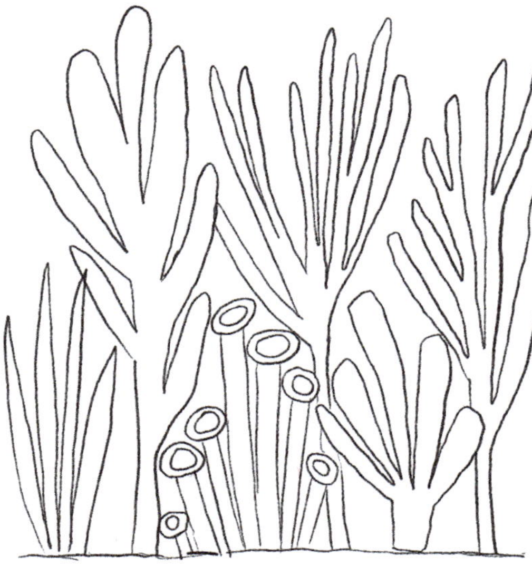

1. Sketch. Using a pencil, lightly sketch the coral reef with various differently shaped corals.

2. Fill the outlines. Paint each coral using a different color from the palette.

3. Add details. Add short brushstrokes and dots to each coral, using the darker value of the coral's base color (by mixing more paint with less water). This creates a sense of depth and shading.

4. Add background. Add some tall filler corals in the background, some blobs of color as a seafloor, and some confetti-like dots in different colors.

Joyful Florals

In this fun floral project, we can skip the sketch and jump right in with watercolors. We'll intuitively paint some fabulous flowers and then add stems, leaves, and smaller buds to round out the final composition. Let's paint some bright flowers with turquoise, peach, and opera pink to create a beautiful spring bouquet!

Medium

Watercolor

Tools and Supplies

- Size 6 round paintbrush

Color Palette

Turquoise blue*

Orange

Opera pink

Peach*

Permanent yellow

Light green

Medium green*

Mixing Instructions

Turquoise blue: Cerulean blue + permanent yellow, then dilute with water

Peach: Dilute orange with water

Medium green: Light green + a little blue

1. Start with three flowers. Paint a brushstroke as a flower center, then paint unfilled outlines of petals around it. Next, paint some small, loose florals at the corners.

2. Add more. Paint a few more flowers in these styles using different colors. Then add some tiny flower buds in orange and yellow. Don't worry about how "realistic" these flowers look.

3. Add green filler. Using both light and medium green, paint long and loose brushstrokes representing leaves and stems between the flowers. These strokes don't have to be perfect; they can just fill in the gaps and connect the buds.

4. Add more filler. This step is all about adding more color! Load your brush with pink and paint some dots randomly throughout the image, representing the joyful energy. You might also fill some color in a petal or two of the central flower.

Orange Blossom

Fruits and flowers are always a popular choice for watercolor painting, so let's paint some! This won't just be a simple painting of an orange—instead, we'll create a well-rounded composition by adding accents to certain elements of the oranges and flower blossoms with a fine-liner pen and some white gouache.

Medium

Gouache

Tools and Supplies

- Size 6 (or your choice) round paintbrush
- Black fine-liner pen

Color Palette

Orange

Peach*

Turquoise blue*

Light green

Dark green*

Pastel pink*

Mixing Instructions

Peach: Orange + white

Turquoise blue: Cerulean blue + permanent yellow + white

Dark green: Light green + blue

Pastel pink: Opera pink + white

1. Start the oranges. Paint four orange circles. To give the oranges a sense of dimension, they shouldn't be entirely solid in color. Mix orange and a little bit of yellow and use varying levels of water with your paints.

2. Add flowers. Paint loose five-petal flowers in turquoise around the circles. Once the petals have dried, paint the center of each flower in yellow.

3. Add leaves. Paint the stems of the oranges in dark green with some light-green leaves. Then paint some leafy branches in both dark and light green, loosely mixed among the oranges and flowers.

4. Add details. With a black pen, sketch some loose outlines around the painted leaves and partial outlines on the oranges and flowers. Add some white dots on the oranges. Finally, paint some pastel-pink dots in any empty spaces, and maybe a pink leaf or two.

Rainbow Joy

Who said painting rainbows is only for kids?

Let out your inner child and focus on the positive energy all the colors exude. After painting the rainbows themselves, we'll add filler elements like lines, dots, and hearts to make the final picture really pop. Painting rainbows can bring the same joy as actually seeing them!

Medium

Watercolor

Tools and Supplies

- Size 6 (or your choice) round paintbrush
- White acrylic paint marker (optional)

Color Palette

- Light blue*
- Ultramarine blue
- Light purple*
- Permanent yellow
- Opera pink
- Peach*
- Orange
- Pastel pink*

Mixing Instructions

Light blue: Dilute cerulean blue with water

Light purple: Dilute purple with water

Peach: Dilute orange with water

Pastel pink: Dilute opera pink with water, or mix with white

1. Start the rainbows. Paint arches/semicircles across the page in different colors, sizes, and shapes.

2. Finish the rainbows. Add two or three smaller arches to each rainbow in different colors. On some rainbows, also paint small lines radiating from the outermost arch to act as little accents.

3. Add filler. Using different colors, paint filler elements in the background between the rainbows, like lines, dots, and hearts. You can also paint stars or any other elements of your choice (I've added stars in step 4, for example).

4. Add detail. Use paint or an acrylic paint marker to add details to the solid-color layers of the rainbows. These can be the same elements you added to the background, or something new!

Sweet Tooth

I wish I had a magic pencil to bring this cake to life, and I'm sure you will too once you've finished painting! Its colors make enjoying a piece of cake seem even sweeter. For now, let's just have fun painting this rainbow-inspired treat with gouache! We'll add details like sprinkles, a plate, and a picturesque cherry on top.

Medium

Gouache

Tools and Supplies

- Size 6 round paintbrush
- Thin liner paintbrush
- Pencil

Color Palette

Ultramarine blue | Powder blue* | Pastel blue*

Permanent yellow | Medium peach* | Medium purple*

Light pink* | Opera pink

Mixing Instructions

Powder blue: Ultramarine blue + white
Pastel blue: Cerulean blue + white
Medium peach: Orange + white
Medium purple: Purple + white
Light pink: Dilute opera pink with water, or mix with white

1. Sketch. Using a pencil, lightly sketch the slice of cake on a plate with a cherry on top.

2. Paint the cake layers. Paint four thick, horizontal brushstrokes in different colors, each representing one colorful layer of cake.

3. Fill out the cake and plate. Paint a pastel-pink layer around the four cake layers for the frosting. Then paint the plate in two different colors of blue.

4. Add detail. Using opera pink, paint the cherry on top and a small, curved shadow next to the bottom right of the cake. Then paint some tiny, short lines all over the cake for sprinkles. You can also add detail to the plate if you'd like.

Feathers

Let's paint some whimsical feathers!

We've painted many different elements of nature so far, so now we'll try a new texture with these wispy, colorful feathers. We'll start with a base layer of loosely blended colors and then add some definition and decoration on top to pull the painting together.

Medium

Watercolor

Tools and Supplies

- Size 6 round paintbrush
- Thin liner paintbrush
- White acrylic paint marker or gel pen
- Black fine-liner pen
- Pencil

Color Palette

Permanent yellow · Opera pink · Peach*

Orange · Light blue* · Purple

Mixing Instructions

Peach: Dilute orange with water

Light blue: Dilute cerulean blue with water

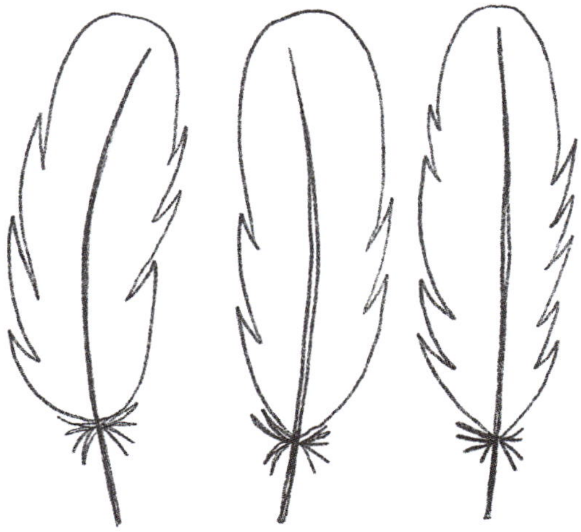

1. Sketch. Using a pencil, lightly sketch three feathers in a row, making each one quite similar to the others. The interest will come through the colors later!

2. Fill in the feather. Fill in each feather using the wet-on-wet technique while leaving a gap for the shaft in the center of the feather. Use multiple colors from the color palette for each feather to make them more whimsical.

3. Paint the shafts. Paint the shafts of the feathers using a liner brush with tiny brushstrokes radiating outward at the base of each feather. Use the same color as the shaft to paint a thin line down the center of each feather.

4. Add detail. Using a white acrylic paint marker or gel pen, add patterning to each feather, like lines, dots, and other creative motifs. Use a black pen to add a rough outline around each feather.

Birds

Let's paint some pretty birds in flight using gouache!

We'll use solid colors and their darker values to paint the birds, carefully accentuate their facial features in purple, and then add fun little accents around them. While you paint, think of the peaceful sound of birds chirping outside your window in the morning.

Medium

Gouache

Tools and Supplies

- Size 6 round paintbrush
- Thin liner paintbrush
- Pencil

Color Palette

Mixing Instructions

Medium purple: Purple + white

Pastel pink: Opera pink + white

Orange yellow: Very little orange + yellow

Coral: Orange + red + white

Medium blue: Cerulean blue + white

1. Sketch. Using a pencil, lightly sketch six or so birds flying in different positions and angles. Add squiggles around them.

2. Paint the bird bodies. Paint each bird in a different solid color from the palette. Don't paint the beaks.

3. Add detail. Using a darker value of each bird's color, draw a rough outline around each bird with a liner brush to refine the feathers and wings. Then paint the eyes and the beaks of the birds in purple.

4. Add background. To add more joy to the painting, paint some curvy lines, like party elements or squiggles, in the gaps between the birds. This makes the painting look more fun and gives it movement.

Easter Eggs

Let's use all the bright colors to paint this one and just have fun. Not picking a color palette before you paint can allow you to become naturally intuitive in choosing colors—try it! We'll paint pretty Easter eggs in solid colors, create some eclectic patterns on them, and finally add some confetti around them to fill in the background.

Medium

Watercolor (or you can use gouache instead)

Tools and Supplies

- Size 6 round paintbrush
- Thin liner paintbrush
- White acrylic paint marker (optional)

Color Palette

- Opera pink
- Permanent yellow
- Periwinkle*
- Peach*
- Light mint green*
- Cerulean blue
- Coral*
- Pastel orange*
- Orange
- Purple
- Ultramarine blue

Mixing Instructions

Periwinkle: Purple + blue, then dilute with water

Peach: Dilute orange with water

Light mint green: Light green + a little cerulean blue + white

Coral: Orange + red + white

Pastel orange: Dilute orange with water

1. Paint the egg shapes. Paint the base layer of the eggs in different colors, with each egg sitting close to or touching the others. Place them at various angles.

2. Add details. Get creative and paint different patterns on each egg with a contrasting color of your choice. It can be simple lines, hearts, stars, dots, or any pattern you can imagine.

3. Add white. With a white acrylic paint marker or gouache, add some more details on the patterns. Get creative and make it interesting!

4. Add background. In the white spaces around the eggs, paint some colorful short lines representing confetti or sprinkles.

Summer Palms

Let's break away from painting the usual green palm trees by incorporating bright summer colors instead! By using various colors, we'll abstract the typical idea of palm trees. Adding detail and definition to the leaves and trunks will enhance the unusual colors and ground the final picture with some elements of realism.

Medium

Watercolor

Tools and Supplies

- Size 6 round paintbrush
- Thin liner paintbrush
- White acrylic paint marker

Color Palette

Mixing Instructions

Teal blue: Ultramarine blue + dark green

Light blue: Dilute cerulean blue with water

Peach: Dilute orange with water

1. Paint trunks. Paint an assortment of medium-width, tall lines using ultramarine blue to represent the trunks of the trees. Make sure to leave enough space between each trunk for the palm leaves next.

2. Paint leaves. Paint the palm leaves radiating up and out from the top of each trunk. For every leaf, use a different color from the palette.

3. Add detail. Add some short, horizontal lines on the trunk of each tree using a darker value of ultramarine blue to create a sense of texture and dimension. Then paint one to three coconuts in peach or teal at the center of every tree.

4. Add white. Add some details, like dots or lines, on the palm leaves using a white acrylic paint marker or gouache.

Teapots

Painting simple household objects might sound boring, but it can be really fun! If you let your creativity flow, you'll end up with a lovely and unique painting. This project will inspire you to have a creative approach to painting other household items like vases, spoons, plates, teacups, and more. Remember: you can always paint beyond the details of what you see.

Medium

Watercolor

Tools and Supplies

- Size 6 round paintbrush
- Thin liner paintbrush
- White acrylic paint marker (optional)
- Pencil

Color Palette

Mixing Instructions

Pastel pink: Opera pink + white

Light blue: Dilute cerulean blue with water

1. Sketch. Using a pencil, lightly sketch four teapots. Give each one a unique shape and details.

2. Paint the shapes. Paint the body, lid, handle, and spout of each teapot using one limited set of colors for each. For example, the blue teapot uses a couple shades of the two blues.

3. Add patterns. Using a contrasting color, paint a different pattern on each teapot. You can fill one teapot with simple lines and dots, another with flowers, etc.

4. Add fine detail. Paint a few dark lines on the handles and lids to give them definition. Using a white acrylic paint marker, add some dots within the patterning and, if you want, a highlight to the mouth of the spout, as in the blue teapot.

Floral Vase

Let's paint an elegant vase with flowers in it!

We'll skip the sketch for this project and jump straight into painting. We'll start with the vase, add some gorgeous flowers, and then add details like stems, buds, and shadows. Notice how beautifully the bold colors in this painting complement each other.

Medium

Watercolor

Tools and Supplies

- Size 6 round paintbrush
- Thin liner paintbrush

Color Palette

Mixing Instructions

Leaf green: Light green + ultramarine blue

Peach: Dilute orange with water

1. Paint the vase. Paint two vases using ultramarine blue. Add more concentrated blue on the left sides, tops, and bottoms to create a sense of dimension in the vases.

2. Add flowers. Paint small, loose flowers in yellow and tiny buds in pink. Float these flowers above the vases.

3. Add greenery. Using a thin liner brush, paint the stems, starting from inside the vases and connecting to the flowers and buds. Then, using a round brush, paint leaf brushstrokes between the flowers.

4. Add detail and a table. Add some light-blue filler buds among the existing buds, then paint some details on the vases using a concentrated blue. Finally, add a peach table under the vases, dragging in a tiny bit of the dark blue to create a sense of shadows.

Juicy Strawberries

It's time to paint some delicious strawberries!

First we'll learn how to paint an individual strawberry in watercolor, incorporating red, pink, and peach colors to make each strawberry jump off the page. Then we'll learn how to combine watercolor and gouache strawberries for a different result using similar techniques. The final painting will have you itching to head to the farmers' market!

Medium

Watercolor and gouache

Tools and Supplies

- Size 6 round paintbrush
- White acrylic paint marker
- Pencil

Color Palette

Mixing Instructions

Reddish pink: Red + opera pink

Peach: Dilute orange with water

Warm orange: Yellow + a little orange or red

Light green: Dark green + a little white

Light purple: Dilute purple with water

This finished piece was painted using gouache, and the individual strawberry steps on the facing page were painted using watercolor.

1. Paint the sides. With red watercolor, paint a curved line, outlining the left side of a strawberry. Then, with reddish pink, paint another curved line starting from the bottom point of the first line to create the shape of the strawberry.

2. Fill the berry. While the paint on both sides is still wet, fill in the center with peach. Then finish the shape of the strawberry by painting the top with warm orange.

3. Add the leaves. Pick a dark-green color and paint the cap of the strawberry with short, medium-width brushstrokes stemming out from the top.

4. Add detail. Using a white acrylic paint marker, add dots to the strawberry to serve as seeds. Now you can adapt this basic strawberry method using different, fewer, or more shades of the colors to create a variety of strawberries!

5. Paint a background. Now let's use what we've learned to make a strawberry composition! First, paint a light-purple background with watercolor to get a washed effect. You could paint the background with gouache if you prefer.

6. Sketch the berries. Sketch a strawberry bunch lightly on top of the background with a pencil or colored pencil.

7. Paint the berries and leaves. Switch to gouache, but use the same technique you learned earlier to paint two strawberries using red and pink. Then paint the stems and leaves in a dark-green gouache shade of your choice.

8. Add detail. With white gouache or a white acrylic paint marker, paint some seeds on the strawberries. Add some white flowers with red centers around them. Mix some light green to add details on the leaves.

Potted Succulent

Let's paint a potted succulent!

There are some really useful tricks in this project that make the final painting look more detailed and realistic. We'll start with a background layer and a sketch, then paint base layers for the plant and its pot, and, finally, finish up with some details and shadows.

Medium

Watercolor

Tools and Supplies

- Size 6 round paintbrush
- Thin liner paintbrush
- Pencil

Color Palette

Mixing Instructions

Light pink: Dilute opera pink with water

Pastel green: Dilute light green with water

Medium green: Light green + dark green

Warm yellow: Yellow + a little orange or red

1. Paint the background. Paint a light background in light pink, using lots of water in your paint mixture.

2. Sketch. Once the background has fully dried, use a pencil to lightly sketch the succulent plant and its pot on top.

3. Paint the leaves. Paint the leaves of the succulent in different hues of green.

4. Paint the pot. Paint the base layer of the pot in warm yellow and orange.

5. Detail the leaves. With a thin liner brush, pick a dark green and paint some short, vertical strokes on all the leaves, resembling the patterns on a snake plant.

6. Add shadows. With a darker hue of orange, paint a rough outline of the pot and some smaller strokes toward the left side of the pot. Then use two darker, muddier shades of pink to add a two-toned shadow at the base of the pot.

Creativity Tip

To make this project more simple and less detailed, you can fill a page with solid-color squares and then paint a simple element on each square, rather than making one large, detailed element like the houseplant featured in this main project. Try choosing a single theme to follow for the page, such as food, fruits, beach elements, or your favorite things. Give it a go—it's so much fun!

Christmas Joy

Let's paint some cheerful Christmas trees in a loose doodle style!

Think outside the box of the typical green Christmas tree and make them super colorful. You can decorate each tree with baubles, tinsel, or anything you'd like. This painting would make a great framed wall hanging, party invitation, or holiday greeting card! Create it in your sketchbook first to get a feel for it and then re-create it separately for its intended purpose.

Medium

Watercolor

Tools and Supplies

- Size 6 round paintbrush
- Thin liner paintbrush

Color Palette

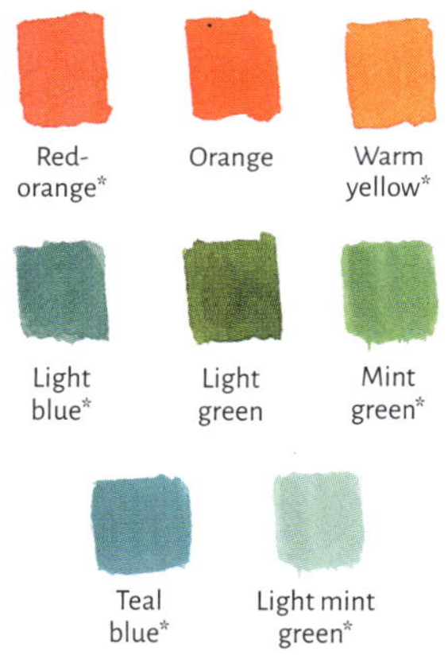

Mixing Instructions

Red-orange: Orange + a little red

Warm yellow: Yellow + a little orange or red

Light blue: Dilute cerulean blue with water

Mint green: Light green + a little cerulean blue

Teal blue: Cerulean blue + green

Light mint green: Light green + a little cerulean blue + white

1. **Paint the trees.** Using different colors from the palette, paint trees in a variety of shapes, sizes, and styles. Get creative—think of different ways to paint a triangle. You'll notice that my trees are made of stacked triangles or lots of lines.

2. **Add ornaments.** Add patterns to each of the Christmas trees. This could be dots, lines, or waves, representing ornaments, strings of lights, or tinsel.

3. **Add stars and trunks.** Add a star to the top of each tree to make them twinkle and a trunk to the base of each tree to ground them.

4. **Add a background.** For a final element of joy, paint some stars and confetti lines scattered around the trees.

Bright Florals

These flowers are such a fun way to fill a page!

They have a more blocky, retro feel than the Joyful Florals project we did earlier. By starting with abstract shapes and using them to drive your composition, you give yourself a little structure within which to have fun with color. Let's paint this field of flowers!

Medium

Watercolor

Tools and Supplies

- Size 6 round paintbrush
- White acrylic paint marker
- Pencil

Color Palette

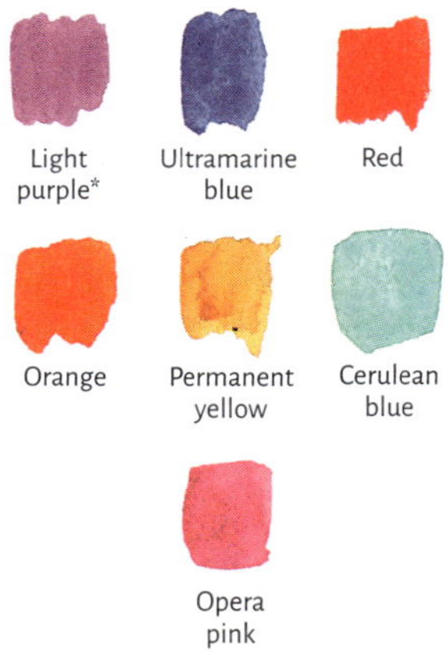

Mixing Instructions

Light purple: Dilute purple with water

1. Sketch shapes. Using a pencil, lightly sketch some abstract shapes—sort of like distorted hexagonal shapes. They should take up most of the area you want to paint, but with a little open space between each one.

2. Sketch flowers. At the center of each shape, draw an oval to represent the center of each flower. Then, sketch petals all the way around each circle, filling the abstract shapes as best you can. Erase your initial abstract shapes before continuing.

3. Paint the flowers. Paint each flower in a different color from the color palette. Depending on how many colors you want to use in total and how many shapes you drew initially, you might repeat a color.

4. Add detail. Paint the center of each flower with a contrasting color from the palette. Using an acrylic paint marker, add white dots to each flower center. In the remaining spaces between the flowers, paint some fun elements like dots or sprinkles.

Colorful Insects

Insects are such an important and underappreciated part of our ecosystem, so let's paint some cute ones in fun colors! We'll start with a sketch, paint their bodies, and then add details to make them more defined and eye-catching. Notice how their different patterns make each of them incredibly unique, even though they're so tiny in real life!

Medium

Watercolor (or you can use gouache instead)

Tools and Supplies

- Size 6 round paintbrush
- Thin liner paintbrush
- White acrylic paint marker
- Pencil

Color Palette

Mixing Instructions

Pastel orange: Dilute orange with water

Coral red: Orange + red

Light purple: Dilute purple with water

Light blue: Dilute cerulean blue with water

Dark periwinkle: Purple + ultramarine blue

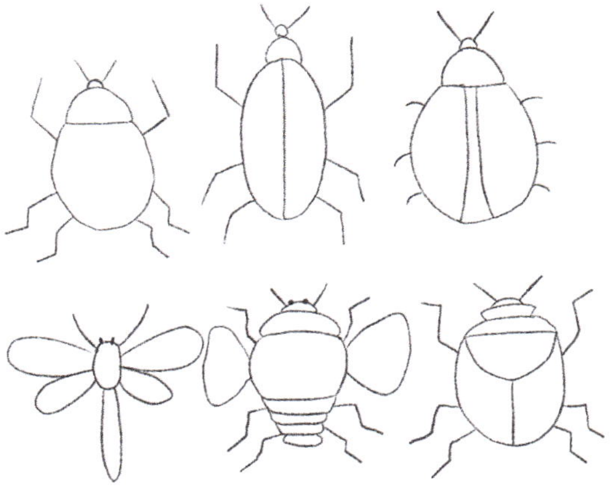

1. Sketch. Using a pencil, lightly sketch six different insects. Give them different body shapes and details.

2. Paint the bodies. Paint the body of each insect in different color combinations from the palette.

3. Add legs. Using a thin liner brush and concentrated dark periwinkle, paint the legs and the antennae of the insects.

4. Add details. With a white acrylic paint marker or white gouache, add patterns to the insects' bodies. You can use lines, dots, and circles. Keep it simple and have fun!

Llama

Let's paint a fluffy llama with extra-colorful details!

We'll add lots of pom-pom strings and a colorful saddle to make the final picture beautiful and bright. This painting would make such an adorable handmade party invite or birthday card if you paint some candles or cake around the llama. Create it in your sketchbook first to get a feel for it and then re-create it separately for its intended purpose.

Medium

Watercolor (or you can use gouache instead)

Tools and Supplies

- Size 6 round paintbrush
- Thin liner paintbrush
- Pencil

Color Palette

Ultramarine blue

Coral red*

Permanent yellow

Peach*

Light blue*

Opera pink

Orange

Mixing Instructions

Coral red: Orange + red

Peach: Dilute orange with water

Light blue: Dilute cerulean blue with water

1. Sketch. Using a pencil, lightly sketch the outline of the llama. Don't forget to sketch its eyes, nose, and mouth, as well as its pom-pom strings and saddle.

2. Paint the body outline. Paint the fluffy body outline with ultramarine blue. Paint the ears, face, legs, and tail of the llama in yellow. Then paint a thin outline of orange around the yellow areas and the hooves in coral red.

3. Add details. With a thin liner brush, paint some pom-poms on string around the neck of the llama. Paint some semicircles on the body of the llama in bright colors to make it look like it has a saddle. Add some simple lines on top to give it a fun pattern.

4. Add a background. Paint a light-blue square background with a very watery paint mixture. Then, to add more fun, paint pom-poms in different colors all around the edges to make it look like a banner or rug.

Roller Skate

Let's get rolling and paint a retro roller skate!

We'll use lots of bright colors like peach, opera pink, and purple and then add fun accents on and around the skate to liven up the final picture. Enjoy the pretty colors and reminisce on your own fun skating memories while you paint!

Medium

Watercolor (or you can use gouache instead)

Tools and Supplies

- Size 6 round paintbrush
- Thin liner paintbrush
- Pencil

Color Palette

Mixing Instructions

Peach: Dilute orange with water

Light blue: Dilute cerulean blue with water

Light purple: Dilute purple with water

1. Sketch. Using a pencil, lightly sketch the outline of the roller skate, including details like the laces, wheels, and toe stop.

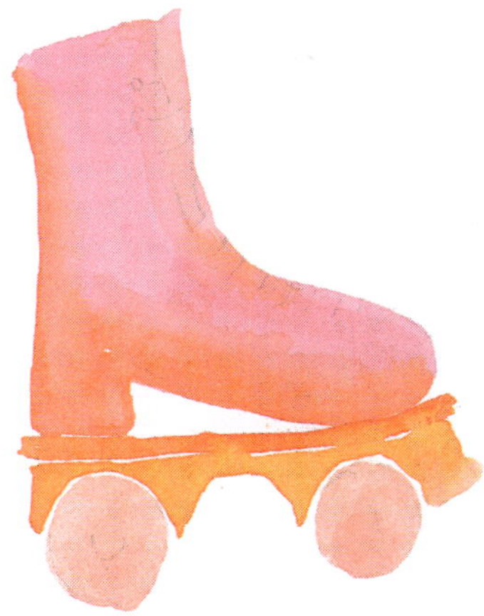

2. Paint the main shape. Paint the body of the roller skate in a gradient of pink, orange, and red. Paint the bottom of the skate in yellow and the wheels in peach.

3. Add details. Using a thin liner brush, paint the lace of the skate in purple. Paint the heel and sole of the skate and outline the wheels with the same color. Then paint a horizontal line across the top of the skate to represent the inside of the boot.

4. Add decoration. Finally, paint some accent elements on either side of the skate, like stars and confetti. You could also paint some stars on the skate or add a quote like "Let's get rolling!"

Lake Swan

This project is a bit more complex than what we've covered so far in the book, but don't worry! With all the practice you've had completing the other projects, you've got the skills to nail it. Remember to have some patience and pay close attention to the serenity of the scene as you put it together. Now let's paint a beautiful lake with an elegant swan, water lilies, and reflective water!

Medium

Watercolor (or you can use gouache instead)

Tools and Supplies

- Size 6 round paintbrush
- Thin liner paintbrush
- White acrylic paint marker (optional)
- Pencil

Color Palette

Medium coral* · Medium yellow* · Peach*

Light blue* · Medium blue* · Ultramarine blue

Pastel green* · Leaf green* · Blush pink*

Opera pink · Orange

Mixing Instructions

Medium coral: Red + orange, then dilute with water

Medium yellow: Dilute permanent yellow with water

Peach: Dilute orange with water

Light blue: Dilute cerulean blue with water

Medium blue: Cerulean blue + ultramarine blue, then dilute with water

Pastel green: Dilute light green with water

Leaf green: Light green + ultramarine blue

Blush pink: Opera pink + a little orange

1. Sketch. Using a pencil, lightly sketch the outline of a swan, cattails, water lilies, and water.

2. Paint the body. Using the wet-on-wet technique, paint the body of the swan in a mix of peach and yellow. Then paint the beak of the swan with orange and the eye area with blue mixed with black or dark gray.

3. Add detail. With a thin liner brush, paint wings and feathers on the body of the swan in orange to make them look more defined.

4. Paint greenery. Switch back to your round brush to paint long leaves to the left of and behind the swan. Use multiple long brushstrokes of pastel green and leaf green. Then, with dark green, add some very thin leaves that are a bit taller.

5. Add cattails. Paint some cattail heads in opera pink, blush pink, and orange on top of the long, thin, green leaf lines.

6. Paint water lilies. Paint each of the water lily flowers in an orange-and-pink combination and then paint each flower's leaf with leaf green.

7. Add detail. Using a thin liner brush, paint some dark-green, small lines on the long leaves and the leaves of the water lilies to give them more definition.

8. Paint the water. Switch back to your round brush to paint the water with light blue using broad brushstrokes, leaving some white gaps. While this light-blue layer is still wet, add some brushstrokes with medium blue.

9. Add detail. Once the previous blues are dry, add some thinner, wavy brushstrokes with ultramarine blue. Finally, to balance the colors of the cattails and lilies, add some tiny lines in pink and orange on the water, making it look like reflections.

10. Add white accents. Using a white acrylic paint marker, add some ripples to the water, including some dots in the mix to make the painting look more whimsical. Sometimes I wonder how such small details can bring such magic to a painting!

Creativity Tip

Try expanding this painting into an entire larger page by painting more swans in different sizes, representing a family. You might also a frog floating on one or two of the lotus leaves, instead of a flower. What other fun pond elements can you think of including?

Seashells

Let's take a colorful twist to seashells and paint them in an abstract brush style with lots of vibrant colors! The first few steps of this project are a bit more intuitive than others, but you have to trust the process. These gorgeous beachy seashells will come together with just a little confidence and patience.

Medium

Gouache

Tools and Supplies

- Size 6 round paintbrush
- White acrylic paint marker or gel pen
- Pencil

Color Palette

Mixing Instructions

Medium pink: Opera pink + white

Turquoise blue: Cerulean blue + permanent yellow + white

Peach: Orange + white

Pastel purple: Purple + white

1. Sketch. Using a pencil, lightly sketch the outline of a collection of seashells in different shapes and sizes. Try to space them evenly near one another.

2. Start with yellow. Paint yellow brushstrokes randomly on a few sections of each of the seashells. Don't fully fill anything—just a few abstract strokes will do.

3. Add pink. Paint medium pink next to and around the yellow, and add some pink brushstrokes in other areas too.

4. Add orange. Now paint some more abstract orange strokes in such a way that it starts to bring out the shapes of the seashells. Start filling in spaces around the yellow and pink you've already painted.

5. Add turquoise. Paint turquoise blue in some parts of the seashells to bring out some vibrancy. This cool turquoise will create the contrast needed to build a sense of dimension in the shells.

6. Add ultramarine. Now, with ultramarine blue, paint brushstrokes that mostly outline the shells but that also bleed onto the surface of them in some spots. This step will add structure and definition to the shells.

7. Add purple. Using pastel purple, fill in some, but not all, of the remaining white spaces you see in the seashells. This step is just to add another pretty color to the painting!

8. Finish with peach. Finally, take a peach color and fill up all the remaining white spaces in the seashells.

9. Add white details. With a white acrylic paint marker, gel pen, or even gouache, add some details like dots and lines on top of all the painted layers. Follow the direction of your existing brushstrokes to maintain the illusion of dimension.

10. Add more definition. Using pink or any other color from the palette, define the seashells more by painting outlines that partially merge with the seashells' shapes. Don't paint outlines all the way around each seashell—just paint a few small sections.

Creativity Tip

Why not try painting these seashells on a darker background, like blue or black? You could also take the technique of this project and apply it to beachy elements other than shells, such as turtles, umbrellas, or starfish. Bring your own interpretation to it!

Camping

Let's paint a cute and colorful camping scene!

We'll paint a camping van surrounded by lush flower bushes and bright palm trees. This project has many steps and requires lots of detailing and layering, but take your time and have fun creating it. This project is also a great way to get accustomed to approaching small yet complex artwork. Soak up the scenery and think back on some fun camping memories while you paint!

Medium

Gouache

Tools and Supplies

- Size 6 round paintbrush
- Thin liner paintbrush
- White acrylic paint marker
- Black fine-liner pen
- Pencil

Color Palette

Turquoise blue*
Medium pink*
Opera pink
Orange
Permanent yellow
Pastel green*
Forest green*
Dark teal*
Brown
Peach*
Gray
Light blue*

Mixing Instructions

Turquoise blue: Cerulean blue + permanent yellow + white

Medium pink: Opera pink + white

Pastel green: Light green + white

Forest green: Mix ultramarine blue and light green

Dark teal: Teal + blue

Peach: Orange + white

Light blue: Cerulean blue + white

1. Sketch. Using a pencil, lightly sketch the camping van, ground, bushes, and palm trees.

2. Paint the van shape. Paint the van's body in peach, the kayak in orange, and the wheels in gray.

3. Paint the ground. Paint the grass underneath the van with both hues of green, along with yellow and a tint of orange.

4. Add flowers. Add some abstract flowers to the ground in turquoise, opera pink, medium pink, orange, and white. These can just be some dots painted close to each other to make it look like bunches of flowers.

5. Paint the sky. Paint a base layer of the sky using light blue. This layer can be watered down to watercolor consistency to get a softer tone. Then, with forest green, paint some tiny bushes on either side of the van, on top of the flower layer.

6. Paint bushes. With pastel green, turquoise, and forest green, paint large bushes on either side of the van. Painting the leaves of the bushes in different colors will create really nice contrast.

7. Paint palm trees. Next, paint the palm leaves in yellow, orange, and medium pink to bring a colorful twist to typically green palm leaves. Paint the trunks of the trees brown.

8. Add detail. Paint some dots and lines on the palm leaves using pink and orange, then add some coconuts too. Add texture lines to the trunks using brown and gray. Next, add some similar details to the bushes using darker forest green and dark teal.

9. Add more flowers. To balance the green bushes and to make the piece overall more colorful, repeat step 4 to add flowers to the bushes on either side of the van.

10. Detail the van. Sketch the doors and window with orange paint and a black pen. Add detail to the kayak with black pen. Add some orange shadows to the front of the van and its windows.

11. Continue detailing the van. Paint the top of the van with medium pink. Add some orange brushstrokes to the bottom of the van. Tint the windows with turquoise blue. Then use a black pen to define the entire structure of the van. You can add black pen sketching to the palm trees too.

12. Finish the van. Paint orange vertical lines on the bottom of the van. Using a white acrylic paint marker, add some white lines to represent the reflections on the glass windows.

Geometric Flowers

Let's take a different approach to painting flowers now by making them geometric. Imagine this as a fusion of sharp geometric shapes and natural flowers. We'll start with the center of each flower and then work our way up to a full page of detailed flowers from there. Let's get started on these interesting and unique florals!

Medium

Watercolor

Tools and Supplies

- Size 6 round paintbrush
- Thin liner paintbrush

Color Palette

Peach*	Orange	Permanent yellow
Medium purple*	Purple	Light blue*
Ultramarine blue	Light green	Dark green

Mixing Instructions

Peach: Dilute orange with water

Medium purple: Dilute purple with water

Light blue: Dilute cerulean blue with water

1. Paint geometric centers. Paint geometric shapes, such as rectangles, hexagons, and squares, in different colors from the palette to create the center of various flowers-to-be.

2. Add petals. Paint the petals of the flowers in geometric shapes with colors that contrast the flower center they are around. You can use a completely different color than the center, or a much-darker or much-lighter value of the same color.

3. Add leaves and stems. Paint the stems and leaves as skinny, elongated rectangles in light green and dark green.

4. Finish the flower centers. Add detail to the center of each flower using dots, lines, and some small rectangles in darker colors.

5. Add some filler. Paint a few geometric filler elements in the spaces between the flowers, stems, and leaves. You can include lines, rectangles, and even small, simple geometric flowers.

6. Add detail to the flowers. Paint more details that connect the center of each flower to its petals, such as overlapping lines. Then add some details at the outer edges of the geometric petals, like simple dots or contrasting-color outlines. Use dark purple or blue, not black.

7. Add detail to the leaves and stems. Use dark green to add details to the stems and leaves. For the stems, you can simply paint some small brushstrokes on top; for the leaves, you can paint on some veins.

8. Finish the background. Paint some more dots in pastel colors to fill in any blank spaces between the flowers. You can add an outline to some of the flowers with a black pen, or even get creative with paint markers to add extra details if you wish.

Simple geometric shapes can also make a cool composition in their own right!

Bright Side

Let's paint a gorgeous, ultra-colorful landscape!

We'll start with a classic blue sky and gradually add various structures and details to end up with a bright and vibrant outdoor scene featuring mountains, trees, and flower patches. You'll also have the option to try out a different art style and outline elements of the picture in white. Let's get started!

Medium

Gouache

Tools and Supplies

- Size 6 round paintbrush
- White acrylic paint marker or gel pen
- Pencil

Color Palette

Mixing Instructions

Powder blue: Ultramarine blue + white

Teal: Ultramarine blue + green

Pastel green: Light green + white

Leaf green: Light green + a little cerulean blue

Peach: Orange + white

Pastel purple: Purple + white

Pastel pink: Opera pink + white

Turquoise blue: Cerulean blue + permanent yellow + white

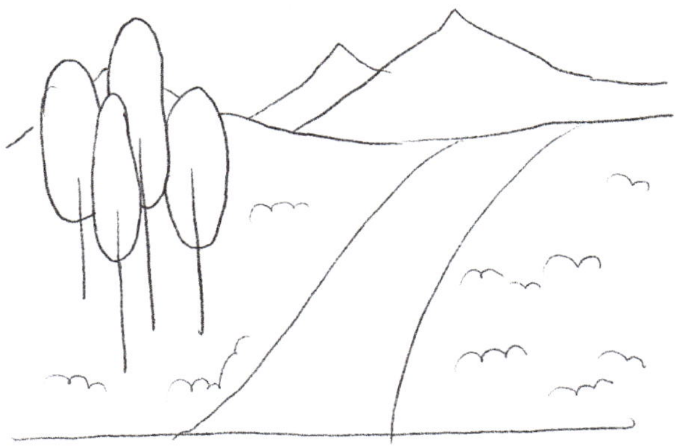

1. Sketch. Using a pencil, lightly sketch the landscape, including mountains, trees, a roadway, and grass.

2. Paint the sky. Paint the sky in powder blue, blending it so that it doesn't look like a solid patch of one single color. You want it to have a gradient effect, so use varying amounts of water and white gouache mixed in.

3. Paint the mountains and trees. Paint the mountains in ultramarine blue and teal blue. Then paint base layers of the trees in different greens from the palette.

4. Paint the ground. Paint the land area in a gradient of peach to orange on the left and of orange to purple on the right, leaving the pathway white. Blend all the colors well while painting to ensure a smooth transition from one color to the next.

5. Paint the road. Paint the pathway in a vibrant mix of colors like opera pink, pastel pink, and orange. Blend the colors well while painting, but make sure not to let them bleed over into the land area.

6. Add detail to the left. On the left side of the land, paint some abstract strokes in orange. Use short, vertical strokes painted close to each other to represent plants. Then paint the trunks of each tree with the same color.

7. Add detail to the right. On the right side of the land, paint some curved, short brushstrokes very close to each other with opera pink, turquoise, white, and orange. Make the patches toward the bottom more defined than toward the top, to create a sense of depth.

8. Finish the ground. Repeat similar brushstrokes from step 7 with teal blue and turquoise, adding them along the edges of the pathway and on both the sides of the land.

9. Add detail to the mountains and trees. Add various colors to the mountains, using short brushstrokes that start from the peaks. Don't completely cover the mountains. Then paint some vertical lines with dark green and turquoise on the left sides of the trees to add dimension.

10. Finish with white accents. Using a white acrylic paint marker or gel pen, add some white details like lines and dots along the pathway, on the mountain, and on the trees.

Creativity Tip

Take what you learned from this project and try painting other landscapes, such as a beach or a tropical landscape, in a similar style. Or why not play with color? You could paint this same landscape in a muted color palette or with pastels instead of the brights featured here. Or really challenge yourself by painting the whole thing in monochromatic colors, similar to the mountains, by adjusting the values of the colors.

Houseplants

Time to paint some pretty houseplants!

We'll use lots of different shades of green, as well as some accent colors, to make each plant pop. Then, we'll have some fun painting the pots with colorful and unique patterns. The final picture will make you want to head over to your local garden center and pick up a new plant!

Medium

Gouache

Tools and Supplies

- Size 6 round paintbrush
- Thin liner paintbrush
- White acrylic paint marker (optional)
- Pencil

Color Palette

Mixing Instructions

Powder blue: Ultramarine blue + white
Peach: Orange + white
Coral: Orange + red + white
Leaf green: Blue + light green
Pastel green: Light green + white

1. Sketch. Using a pencil, lightly sketch a set of three shelves with three plant pots on each one. Use a variety of pot shapes as well as plant shapes.

2. Paint the shelves. Paint the three shelves each in a different color: permanent yellow, cerulean blue, and opera pink.

3. Paint the pots. Paint the pots in different colors from the color palette. If you wish, you may also use two colors to paint a single pot.

4. Start with pastel-green leaves. Paint two or more leaves of each plant in pastel green.

5. Add light-green leaves. Paint two or more leaves of each plant in light green.

6. Finish with leaf-green leaves. Paint the remaining leaves of each plant in leaf green.

7. Add flowers. Paint some flowers in pink, yellow, and peach on the various plants, and also add some leaves in these colors. This will create nice pops of color throughout.

8. Add detail to the plants. With a thin liner brush and ultramarine blue, paint the stem and veins for every plant. Then, with the same color, paint a thin line representing a shadow under the foliage, right above the pot, on some of the plants.

9. Add detail to the pots. Using a white acrylic paint marker or white gouache, draw patterns on each pot. These can be lines, dots, diamonds, zigzags, or whatever you like. Try painting a different pattern on every pot!

10. Add shading to the shelves. Add a layer of shadow on top of each shelf right underneath the pots using a darker, contrasting color.

Creativity Tip

This project concept is just perfect for painting a bookshelf! You can even include a small houseplant or two mixed in among the book spines. Or try "zooming out": paint a simple living-room scene that includes a bookshelf along the back wall with a cozy sofa in front of it.

Loose Florals

This is a lovely capstone project to the book! It will teach you how to create several styles of individual flowers so that you can scatter them across a full page in a lovely, loose, organic manner. After taking some time to learn and practice these individual elements, you can have so much fun incorporating them everywhere!

Medium

Watercolor

Tools and Supplies

- Size 6 round paintbrush
- Thin liner paintbrush

Color Palette

Mixing Instructions

Coral red: Orange + red
Peach: Dilute orange with water
Light blue: Dilute cerulean blue with water
Medium blue: Cerulean blue + white
Medium green: Light green + dark green
Medium purple: Dilute purple with water

)range Flower

Paint the petals. Start with a brushstroke that is curved to e left, add two straight brushstrokes next to it, and finish with orushstroke that is curved to the right.

Add orange. While the painted petals are still wet, drop ›me orange into them, letting it bleed and blend organically.

3. **Paint the stem and leaves.** With medium or light green, paint the stem and the leaves directly below the flower.

4. **Add dark green.** While the painted stem and leaves are still wet, drop some dark green into them, letting it bleed and blend organically.

lue Filler

Paint the stems. Start by king a gray or grayish-blue lor and painting a treelike ınch of delicate, thin, long ems that collect at the ›ttom and spread out at e top.

Add flowers. With light ue, paint some abstract ›ts on the "branches" of the ee."

Add more flowers. With edium blue, paint some ore abstract dots on e "tree," making sure to 'erlap some of the existing ;ht-blue dots.

Purple Flower

1. Paint the petals. Paint one vertical, pointed petal in medium purple, then paint another pointed petal tilted on either side of it. Add a drop of dark purple in the center to connect them.

2. Add a stem. Paint the stem of the flower in dark green.

3. Add leaves. With the same dark green, paint some loose leaves and some random, thin brushstrokes next to or touching the stem and leaves.

4. Add detail. To add more character, paint some abstract dots in light green around the leaves. Then, after the flower has dried, paint some abstract dots in diluted purple on top of the flower.

Loose Leaves

1. Paint stems. Start by painting a set of thin, slightly curved brushstrokes to represent the stems and branches of the leaves. Use dark or medium green.

2. Paint leaves. With medium green, paint a few loose leaves, some of which are connected to the stems and some of which are not.

3. Add more substance. With dark green, paint more loose leaves in between the medium-green leaves. Also add some abstract dots around the entire leafy branch.

oral Flower

Paint the petals. Start with two straight brushstrokes in ach. Add a curved brushstroke on either side of these with ral red.

Add a stem. With both dark and medium green, paint a em.

3. **Add leaves.** With dark green, medium green, and light green, paint some loose leaves connected to the stem.

4. **Add detail.** To add more character, paint some abstract dots in light green around the leaves. Then, after the flower has dried, paint some abstract dots in diluted coral red on top of the flower.

Just look at what you can make with these loose florals! Turn to page 115 to see this composition in full.

You don't always have to fill your entire sketchbook page! Here is an example where I created balance and contrast by painting a row of flowers along the bottom half of the paper, but leaving white space above them to let them breathe. It's so simple, but so nice!

lay with flowers of different sizes to create a pleasing omposition. Include a few stray brushstrokes mixed into e background to imply tiny buds.

y an artsy effect by drawing dividing lines to create ctions on a spread of your sketchbook, then drawing a fferent kind of flower in each section.

I love the jewel tones of this loose floral page!

birds

3 TAKING YOUR SKETCHBOOKING FURTHER

In this final section of the book, I'd like to take a moment to discuss some ways you can encourage yourself to set up a successful daily creative practice, and I'd also like to share 100 sketchbook prompts for you to use as you branch out and away from the projects in this book!

Steps to Starting a Daily Painting Practice

If you haven't already started a daily practice, what's holding you back? Read through my tips and recommendations here to see how you can set yourself up for success.

Set a Schedule

Choose a specific amount of time you want to dedicate to your creative sketchbook each day, even if it's just 15 or 30 minutes. Consistency is key to developing a habit. This doesn't have to be on a fixed schedule—you can work in your sketchbook whenever works for you—but if you do tie it to an existing daily habit of yours, you might have better luck making the habit stick. Try it after your morning coffee or your evening walk!

Create a Comfortable Space

Designate a space for your painting practice, whether it's a corner of a room or a portable setup—or maybe even sitting on a garden bench and painting in nature. Make it a space you want to be in.

Choose Prompts

Instead of pressuring yourself to create something from nothing, use simple prompts or themes to guide your daily painting. Prompts provide focus and inspiration. They could be based on objects around you, on nature, or on imaginative concepts. Feel free to refer to the 100 prompts provided on page 120!

Experiment Freely

Allow yourself to paint without judgment. Experiment with colors, techniques, and styles. Remember that your sketchbook is your ultimate playground to play, be creative, and practice without any expectations. This is truly a space where you can tap into your creative joy and channel the creative energy that wants to flow through you.

Stay Inspired

Look for inspiration in everyday life, nature, or art from other artists. This can help keep your creativity flowing and motivate you to explore new themes. You could create a saved folder, Pinterest board, or physical collection of things that inspire you, and refer to it whenever you're feeling low on natural inspiration.

One last note: If you choose to share your art with the world, I encourage you to share from a place of joy and gratitude, for the opportunity it gives you to express yourself, rather than focusing on content creation or gaining followers.

Trust me—when you come from a pure place of joy and set aside expectations, all the goodness that is meant for you will unfold in your life, often in surprising ways. While it's natural to have some expectations, over time they can cloud the joy of your creative experience. So I urge you to simply share your art and show up authentically!

100 Sketchbook Ideas

These 100 prompts encourage the exploration of many diverse themes. Designed to spark your creative joy without the need for hours spent scrolling through Pinterest, they focus on everyday objects and invite your imagination to take the lead.

As you explore colors and shapes in simple yet meaningful ways, you'll find yourself blending the ordinary with the extraordinary. This magical time spent painting will result in unique and vibrant artworks that reflect your personal style, infusing your artistic journey with joy and inspiration.

I would love to see what you create from these prompts. Please share with me on Instagram by tagging me (@viddhi.saschit) or by using the hashtag #creativesketchbookmagic.

Happy painting!

Summer Fruits

Favorite Cocktail Recipe

Peacock

Summer Beach Vibes

Color Swatches

Summer Flowers

Floating in the Pool

Funky Sunglasses

Tropical Fruit Bowl

Umbrella

Colorful Fishes

Lemon Blossom

Sunflower

Sweet Dreams

Radiating Sunlight

Party Balloons

Disco Balls

Birthday Candles

Quilt Pattern

Sea Turtles

Whale

Colorful Cars

Favorite Quote

Coffee Mug

Trees

Autumn Flowers

Whimsical Mushrooms

Pumpkin Patch

Holiday Cookies

Rainbow & Clouds

Flying Kite

Open Window

Cute Sparrows

Colorful Row House

Flower Garden

Playful Dogs

Abstract Brushstrokes

Colorful Bows

Snowflakes

Unicorn

- Ice Cream Cone
- Flower Bouquet
- Colorful Stationery
- Birthday Hats
- Cupcakes
- Bakery Shop
- Ice Cream Truck
- Gardening Essentials
- Vegetables
- Easter Bunnies
- Colorful Snails
- Flower Valley
- Rainbow Mountain
- Dreamy Sunset
- Cozy Cottage
- Surfboards
- Starry Night Sky
- Blooming Roses
- Smiley Emojis
- Favorite Flower
- Favorite Dessert
- Art Supplies
- Beach Essentials
- Misty Pines
- Birthday Elephant
- Fancy Teacups
- Woodland Animal
- Christmas Candies
- Dreamy Mermaid
- All Things Favorite

Shooting Stars	Block Art	Picnic Basket	Retro Camera	Cozy Sweater
Picnic Day	Holiday Ornaments	Merry Snowman	Funky Patterns	Dream Catcher
Sparkling Gems	Festive Lanterns	Colorful Flamingo	Crisp Fall Leaves	Charming Lighthouses
Flower Crown	Colorful Door	Vibrant Fireflies	Cheerful Cacti	Magical Forest
Playful Penguins	Party Dinosaurs	Hot-Air Balloons	Starfish	Parakeet
Folk-Art Bird	Folk-Art Florals	Windmill	Ladybug	Bird on Branch

Index

Note: Page numbers in *italics* indicate projects.